The
DANGEROUS DUTY
of
DELIGHT

LifeChange Books

JOHN PIPER

Multnomah® Publishers *Sisters, Oregon*

THE DANGEROUS DUTY OF DELIGHT
published by Multnomah Publishers, Inc.

© 2001 by Desiring God Foundation
International Standard Book Number: 1-57673-883-3

Cover design by David Carlson Design
Cover image by Photodisc

Italics added in Scripture are the author's emphasis.

Unless otherwise indicated, Scripture quotations are from:
New American Standard Bible © 1960, 1977, 1995
by the Lockman Foundation. Used by permission.
Also quoted: *Revised Standard Version Bible* (RSV) © 1946, 1952 by the Division of
Christian Education of the National Council of the Churches of Christ
in the United States of America
The Holy Bible, New International Version (NIV) © 1973, 1984 by International Bible
Society, used by permission of Zondervan Publishing House.

Multnomah is a trademark of Multnomah Publishers, Inc.,
and is registered in the U.S. Patent and Trademark Office.
The colophon is a trademark of Multnomah Publishers, Inc.

Printed in the United States of America

For information:
MULTNOMAH PUBLISHERS, INC. • P. O. BOX 1720 • SISTERS, OR 97759

Library of Congress Cataloging-in-Publication Data:

Piper, John, 1946–
    The dangerous duty of delight / by John Piper.
        p. cm.
Includes bibliographical references.
ISBN 1-57673-883-3
1. God—Worship and love. I. Title
BV4817.P55 2001
248.4—dc21   2001003826
                05 06 07 08 09 — 15 14 13 12 11 10

Table of Contents

Picture me with my ground teeth stalking joy—
fully armed too, as it's a highly dangerous quest.

FLANNERY O'CONNOR

*Fifteen years ago I dedicated
the longer version of this book,*
DESIRING GOD,
to my father

William Solomon Hottle Piper

*Now, more than ever, there is a sweet indebtedness
I feel to him and the happy holiness
he has lived for the glory of God and for my sake
all these fifty-five years of my life.*

Our hearts are restless until they find their rest in Thee.

SAINT AUGUSTINE

*If I find in myself a desire which no
experience in this world can satisfy,
the most probable explanation is that
I was made for another world.*

C. S. LEWIS

PREFACE

Dear Reader,

I write this little book because the truth and beauty of Jesus Christ, the Son of God, are breathtaking. I say with the ancient psalmist,

> *One thing have I asked of the LORD,*
> *that will I seek after;*
> *that I may dwell in the house of the LORD*
> *all the days of my life,*
> *to behold the beauty of the LORD,*
> *and to inquire in His temple.*

PSALM 27:4, RSV

If you are a guide on a sightseeing trip, and you know that the people are longing to enjoy beauty—even willing to risk their lives to see it—and you come upon some breathtaking ravine, then you should show it to them and urge them to enjoy it. Well, the human race does in fact crave the experience of awe and wonder. And there is no reality more breathtaking than Jesus Christ. He is not safe, but He is stunning.

God has put eternity in man's mind and filled the human heart with longing. But we know not what we long for until we see the breathtaking God. This is the cause of universal restlessness. Hence the famous prayer of Saint Augustine: "You made us for yourself and our hearts find no peace till they rest in you."[1]

> *There is no reality more breathtaking than Jesus Christ.*

The world has an inconsolable longing. It tries to satisfy the longing with scenic vacations, accomplishments of creativity, stunning cinematic productions, sexual exploits, sports extravaganzas, hallucinogenic drugs, ascetic rigors, managerial excellence, etc. But the longing remains. What does this mean? C. S. Lewis answers:

> If I find in myself a desire which no experience in this world can satisfy, the most probable explanation is that I was made for another world.[2]

The tragedy of the world is that the echo is mistaken for the Original Shout. When our back is to the breathtaking beauty of God, we cast a shadow on the earth and fall in love with it. But it does not satisfy.

> The books or the music in which we thought the beauty was located will betray us if we trust to them…. For they are not the thing itself; they are only the scent of a flower we have not found, the echo of a tune we have not heard, news from a country we have never yet visited.[3]

I have written this book because the breathtaking Beauty *has* visited us. "And the Word became flesh, and dwelt among us, and we saw His glory, glory as of the only begotten from the Father, full of grace and truth" (John 1:14). How can I not cry, *Look! Believe! Be satisfied!* It may cost you your life to see it. But it will be worth it, because we know on good authority that "The steadfast love of the LORD is better than life" (Psalm 63:3, RSV). Infinite delight is a dangerous duty. But you will not regret the pursuit. I call it Christian Hedonism.

Chapter 1

TREATING DELIGHT
AS DUTY IS
CONTROVERSIAL

"Christian Hedonism" is a controversial name for an old-fashioned way of life.

It goes back to *Moses,* who wrote the first books of the Bible and threatened terrible things if we would not be happy: "Because you did not serve the LORD your God with joy and a glad heart...therefore you shall serve your enemies" (Deuteronomy 28:47–48).

...and to the Israelite king *David,* who called God his "exceeding joy" (Psalm 43:4); and said, "Serve the LORD with gladness" (Psalm 100:2); and "Delight yourself in the LORD" (Psalm 37:4); and who prayed, "Satisfy us in the morning with Your lovingkindness, that we may…be glad all our days" (Psalm 90:14); and who promised that complete and lasting pleasure is found in God alone: "In Your presence is fullness of joy; in Your right hand there are pleasures forever" (Psalm 16:11).

…and to *Jesus,* who said, "Blessed are you when people insult you…. Rejoice and be glad, for your reward in heaven is great" (Matthew 5:11–12); and who said, "I have spoken to you so that My joy may be in you, and that your joy may be made full" (John 15:11); and who endured the Cross "for the joy set before Him" (Hebrews 12:2); and who promised that, in the end, faithful servants would hear the words, "Enter into the joy of your master" (Matthew 25:21).

"Christian Hedonism" is a controversial name for an old-fashioned way of life.

…and to *James* the brother of Jesus, who said, "Consider it all joy…when you encounter various trials" (James 1:2).

…and to the apostle *Paul,* who was "sorrowful yet always rejoicing" (2 Corinthians 6:10); and who described the ministry of his team as being "workers with you for your joy" (2 Corinthians 1:24); and who commanded Christians to "rejoice in the Lord always" (Philippians 4:4);

and even to "exult in...tribulations" (Romans 5:3).

...and to the apostle *Peter*, who said, "To the degree that you share the sufferings of Christ, keep on rejoicing, so that also at the revelation of His glory you may rejoice with exultation" (1 Peter 4:13).

...and to *Saint Augustine*, who, in the year 386, found his freedom from lust and lechery in the superior pleasures of God. "How sweet all at once it was for me to be rid of those fruitless joys which I had once feared to lose!... You drove them from me, you who are the true, the sovereign joy. You drove them from me and took their place, you who are sweeter than all pleasure."[4]

...and to *Blaise Pascal*, who saw that "all men seek happiness. This is without exception. Whatever different means they employ, they all tend to this end.... The will never takes the least step but to this object. This is the motive of every action of every man, even of those who hang themselves."[5]

...and to the *Puritans* whose aim was to know God so well that "delighting in him, may be the work of our lives,"[6] because they knew that this joy would "arm us against the assaults of our spiritual enemies and put our mouths out of taste for those pleasures with which the tempter baits his hooks."[7]

...and to *Jonathan Edwards*, who discovered and

taught as powerfully as anyone that "the happiness of the creature consists in rejoicing in God, by which also God is magnified and exalted."[8] "The end of the creation is that the creation might glorify [God]. Now what is glorifying God, but a rejoicing at that glory he has displayed?"[9]

...and to *C. S. Lewis,* who discovered "We are far too easily pleased."[10]

...and to a thousand *missionaries,* who have left everything for Christ and in the end have said, with David Livingstone, "I never made a sacrifice."[11]

Christian Hedonism is not new.

So if Christian Hedonism is old-fashioned, why is it so controversial? One reason is that it insists that joy is not just the spin-off of obedience to God, but *part of* obedience. It seems as though people are willing to let joy be a by-product of our relationship to God, but not an essential part of it. People are uncomfortable saying that we are duty-bound to pursue joy.

They say things like, "Don't pursue joy; pursue obedience." But Christian Hedonism responds, "That's like saying, 'Don't eat apples; eat fruit.'" Because joy *is* an act of obedience. We are *commanded* to rejoice in God. If obedience is doing what God commands, then joy is not merely the spin-off of obedience, it *is* obedience. The Bible tells us over and over to pursue joy: "Be glad in the LORD and rejoice, you righteous ones; and shout for joy, all you who are upright in heart" (Psalm 32:11). "Let the nations be glad and sing for joy" (Psalm 67:4). "Delight yourself in the LORD" (Psalm 37:4). "Rejoice that your names are recorded in heaven" (Luke 10:20). "Rejoice in the Lord always; again I will say, rejoice!" (Philippians 4:4).

The Bible does not teach that we should treat delight as a mere by-product of duty. C. S. Lewis got it right when he wrote to a friend, "It is a Christian duty, as you know, for everyone to be as happy as he can."[12] Yes, that is risky and controversial. But it is strictly true. Maximum happiness, both qualitatively and quantitatively, is precisely what we are duty-bound to pursue.

One wise Christian described the relationship between duty and delight this way:

> Suppose a husband asks his wife if he must kiss her good night. Her answer is, "You must, but not that kind of a must." What she means is this: "Unless a spontaneous affection for my person motivates you, your overtures are stripped of all moral value."[13]

In other words, if there is no pleasure in the kiss, the duty of kissing has not been done. Delight in her person, expressed in the kiss, is part of the duty, not a by-product of it.

But if that is true—if delight in doing good is part of what doing good *is*—then the pursuit of pleasure is part of the pursuit of virtue. You can see why this starts to get controversial. It's the seriousness of it all. "You really mean this?" someone says. "You really mean that *hedonism* is not just a trick word to get our attention. It actually says something utterly, devastatingly true about the way we should live. The pursuit of pleasure really is a necessary part of being a good person." That's right. I mean it. The Bible means it. God means it. It is very serious. We are not playing word games.

Let it be crystal clear: We are always talking about joy *in God*. Even joy in doing good is finally joy in God, because the ultimate good that we always aim at is displaying the glory of God and expanding our own joy in God to others. Any other joy would be qualitatively insufficient for the longing of our souls and quantitatively too short for our eternal need. In God alone is *fullness* of joy and joy *forever*.

"In Your presence is *fullness* of joy; in Your right hand there are pleasures *forever*" (Psalm 16:11).

> *Maximum happiness, both qualitatively and quantitatively, is precisely what we are duty-bound to pursue.*

Chapter 2

GLORIFY GOD BY ENJOYING HIM FOREVER

Maximizing our joy in God is what we were created for. "But wait a minute," someone says, "what about the glory of God? Didn't God create us for *His* glory? But here you are saying that He created us to pursue *our* joy!" Which is it? Are we created for His glory or our joy?

Oh how passionately I agree that God created us for His glory! Yes! Yes! God is the most God-centered person in the universe. This is the heartbeat of everything I preach and write. This is what Christian Hedonism is designed to preserve and pursue! God's chief end is to glorify God. This is written all over the Bible. It is the aim of all God does.

God's goal at every stage of creation and salvation is to magnify His glory. You can magnify with a microscope or with a telescope. A microscope magnifies by making tiny things look bigger than they are. A telescope magnifies by making gigantic things (like stars), which look tiny, appear more as they really are. God created the universe to magnify His glory the way a telescope magnifies stars. Everything He does in our salvation is designed to magnify the glory of His grace like this.

Take, for example, some of the steps of our salvation: predestination, creation, incarnation, propitiation, sanctification, and consummation. At every step the Bible says God is doing these things, through Jesus Christ, to display and magnify His glory.

God created you so that you might spend eternity glorifying Him by enjoying Him forever.

- *Predestination:* "He *predestined* us to adoption as sons through Jesus Christ to Himself, according to the kind intention of His will, *to the praise of the glory* of His grace" (Ephesians 1:5–6).
- *Creation:* "Bring My sons from afar and My daughters from the ends of the earth,

everyone who is called by My name, and whom I have created *for My glory*" (Isaiah 43:6–7).

- *Incarnation:* "Christ has become a servant to the circumcision on behalf of the truth of God to confirm the promises given to the fathers, and for the Gentiles *to glorify God* for His mercy" (Romans 15:8–9).

- *Propitiation:*[14] "God displayed [Christ] publicly as a propitiation in His blood through faith. *This was to demonstrate His righteousness*, because in the forbearance of God He passed over the sins previously committed" (Romans 3:25).

- *Sanctification:* "And this I pray, that your love may abound still more and more...having been filled with the fruit of righteousness which comes through Jesus Christ, *to the glory and praise of God*" (Philippians 1:9, 11).

- *Consummation:* "[Those who do not obey the gospel] will pay the penalty of eternal destruction, away from the presence of the Lord and from the glory of His power, when He comes *to be glorified* in His saints on that day, and *to be marveled at* among all who have believed" (2 Thessalonians 1:9–10).

So I could not agree more with the person who says, "God created us and saves us for *His* glory!"

"Well, then," my friend asks, "how can you say that the

aim of life is to maximize our joy? Didn't God create us to share His ultimate aim—to glorify Himself? Which is it? Are we created for His glory or for our joy?"

Here we are at the heart of Christian Hedonism! If you get anything, get this. I learned it from Jonathan Edwards, C. S. Lewis, and, most importantly, from the apostle Paul.

Edwards was the greatest pastor-theologian that America has ever produced. He wrote a book in 1755 called *The End for Which God Created the World.* The foundation and aim of that book is the following stunning insight. It is the deepest basis of Christian Hedonism. Read this old-fashioned English slowly to see Edwards's brilliant resolution.

> *God is glorified not only by His glory's being seen, but by its being rejoiced in.* When those that see it delight in it, God is more glorified than if they only see it. His glory is then received by the whole soul, both by the understanding and by the heart. God made the world that He might communicate, and the creature receive, His glory; and that it might [be] received both by the mind and heart. He that testifies his idea of God's glory [doesn't] glorify God so much as he that testifies also his...delight in it. [15]

This is the solution. Did God create you for *His* glory or for *your* joy? Answer: He created you so that you might spend eternity glorifying Him by enjoying Him forever. In other words, you do not have to choose between glorifying God and enjoying God. Indeed you dare not choose. If you forsake one, you lose the other. Edwards is absolutely right: *"God is glorified not only by His glory's being seen, but by its being rejoiced in."* If we do not rejoice in God, we do not glorify God as we ought.

Here is the rock-solid foundation of Christian Hedonism: *God is most glorified in us when we are most satisfied in Him.* This is the best news in the world. God's passion to be glorified and my passion to be satisfied are not at odds.

You might turn your world on its head by changing one word in your creed—for example, changing *and* to *by*. The old Westminster Catechism asks, "What is man's chief end?" It answers: "Man's chief end is to glorify God *and* enjoy Him forever."

And?

Are glorifying God and enjoying God two distinct things?

Evidently the old pastors who wrote the catechism didn't think they were talking about two things. They said "chief end," not "chief ends." Glorifying God and enjoying Him were one end in their minds, not two.

The aim of Christian Hedonism is to show why this is so. It aims to show that we glorify God *by* enjoying Him forever. This is the essence of Christian Hedonism. *God is most glorified in us when we are most satisfied in Him.*

Perhaps you see now what drives me to be radical about this. If it is true, that God is most glorified in us when we are most satisfied in Him, then look at what is at stake in our pursuit of joy. The glory of God is at stake! If I say that pursuing joy is not essential, I am saying that glorifying God is not essential. But if glorifying God is ultimately important, then pursuing the satisfaction that displays His glory is ultimately important.

Christian Hedonism is not a game. It is what the whole universe is about.

The radical implication is that pursuing pleasure in God is our highest calling. It is essential to all virtue and all reverence. Whether you think of your life vertically in relation to God or horizontally in relation to man, the pursuit of pleasure in God is crucial, not optional. We will see shortly that genuine love for people and genuine worship toward God hang on the pursuit of joy.

Before I saw these things in the Bible, C. S. Lewis snagged me when I wasn't looking. I was standing in Vroman's Bookstore on Colorado Avenue in Pasadena, California, in the fall of 1968. I picked up a thin blue copy of Lewis's book *The Weight of Glory*. The first page changed my life.

> If there lurks in most modern minds the notion that to desire our own good and earnestly to hope for the enjoyment of it is a bad thing, I submit that this notion has crept in from Kant and the Stoics and is no part of the Christian faith. Indeed, if we consider the unblushing promises of reward and the staggering nature of the rewards promised in the Gospels, it would seem that our Lord finds our desires not too strong, but too weak. We are half-hearted creatures, fooling about with drink and sex and ambition when infinite joy is offered us, like an ignorant child who wants to go on making mud pies in a slum because he cannot imagine what is meant by the offer of a holiday at the sea. We are far too easily pleased.[16]

Never in my life had I heard anyone say that the problem with the world was *not* the intensity of our pursuit of happiness, but the *weakness* of it. Everything in me shouted, *Yes! That's it!* There it was in black and white, and to my mind it was totally compelling: The great problem with human beings is that we are far too easily pleased. We don't seek pleasure with nearly the resolve and passion that we should. And so we settle for mud pies of appetite instead of infinite delight.

Lewis said, "We are far too easily pleased." Almost all of Christ's commands are motivated by "the unblushing promises of reward." Based on "the staggering nature of the rewards promised in the Gospels, it would seem that our Lord finds our desires not too strong, but too weak."

Yes. But what does that have to do with the praise and glory of God? Christian Hedonism says that not only must we pursue the joy that Jesus promises, but also that God Himself is glorified in this pursuit. Lewis helped me see this too.

There was another explosive page, this time from his book *Reflections on the Psalms*. Here he showed that the very nature of praise is the consummation of joy in what we admire.

> The most obvious fact about praise—whether of God or anything—strangely escaped me.... I had never noticed that all enjoyment spontaneously overflows into praise...lovers praising their mistresses, readers their favorite poet, walkers praising the countryside.... My whole, more general, difficulty about the praise of God depended on my absurdly denying to us, as regards the supremely Valuable, what we delight to do, what indeed we cannot help doing, about everything else we value.

I think we delight to praise what we enjoy because the praise not merely expresses but completes the enjoyment.[17]

Pursuing joy in God and praising God are not separate acts.

So Lewis helped me put it all together. Pursuing joy in God and praising God are not separate acts. "Praise not merely expresses but completes the enjoyment." Worship is not added to joy, and joy is not the by-product of worship. Worship is the valuing of God. And when this valuing is intense, it is joy in God. Therefore the essence of worship is delight in God, which displays His all-satisfying value.

The apostle Paul clinched my Christian Hedonism with his testimony in Philippians 1. Here is the clearest biblical statement that God is most glorified in us when we are most satisfied in Him. From his imprisonment in Rome he writes:

My earnest expectation and hope [is] that I will not be put to shame in anything, but that with all boldness, Christ will even now, as always, be exalted in my body, whether by life or by death. For to me, to live is Christ and to die is gain. (Philippians 1:20–21)

So his aim is that Christ be "exalted" or "magnified" or "glorified" in his body. He wants this to happen whether he lives or dies. In life and death his mission is to magnify Christ—to show that Christ is magnificent, to glorify Christ, to demonstrate that He is great. That's clear from verse 20—that Christ "shall be exalted in my body, whether by life or by death." The question is: *How* did he expect that to come about?

He shows us the answer in verse 21: "For to me, to live is Christ and to die is gain." Notice how "live" and "die" in verse 21 correspond to "life" and "death" in verse 20. And the connection between the two verses is that verse 21 shows the basis of magnifying Christ by living and dying.

Verse 20	Verse 21
Christ will be exalted.	because for me
whether by my life.	to live is Christ
or my death.	and to die is gain

Consider first the pair, "death" (verse 20) and "die" (verse 21): Christ may be exalted in my body by my death because for me to die is gain. Ponder that. Christ will be exalted in my dying, if dying for me is gain. Do you see what this means about the way Christ is magnified? Christ is magnified by Paul's dying if Paul's dying is experienced as gain.

Why is that? It's because Christ Himself is the gain. Verse 23 makes this clear: "[My] desire [is] to depart [that is, to die] and be *with Christ,* for that is very much better." That is what death does for Christians: It takes us into more intimacy with Christ. We depart and we are with Christ, and that is gain. And when you experience death this way, Paul says, Christ is exalted in your body. Experiencing Christ as gain in your dying magnifies Christ. It is the essence of worship in the hour of death.

If you want to glorify Christ in your dying, you must experience death as gain. Which means Christ must be your prize, your treasure, your joy. He must be a satisfaction so deep that when death takes away everything you love—but gives you more of Christ—you count it gain. When you are satisfied with Christ in dying, He is gloried in your dying.

It's the same with life. We magnify Christ in life, Paul says, by experiencing Christ as our all-surpassing treasure. That's what he means in verse 21 when he says, "For to me, to live is Christ." We know this because in Philippians 3:8 Paul says, "I count all things to be loss in view of the surpassing value of knowing Christ Jesus my Lord, for whom I have suffered the loss of all things, and count them but rubbish so that I may gain Christ."

So Paul's point is that life and death, for a Christian, are acts of worship—they exalt Christ and magnify Him and reveal and express His greatness—when they come from an inner experience of treasuring Christ as gain. Christ is praised in death by being prized above life. And Christ is most glorified in life when we are most satisfied in Him even before death.

The common denominator between living and dying is that Christ is the all-satisfying treasure that we embrace whether we live or die. Christ is praised by being prized. He is magnified as a glorious treasure when He becomes our unrivaled pleasure. So if we are going to praise Him and magnify Him, we dare not be indifferent as to whether we prize Him and find pleasure in Him. If Christ's honor is our passion, the pursuit of pleasure in Him is our duty.

> *If Christ's honor is our passion, the pursuit of pleasure in Him is our duty.*

Chapter 3

AFFECTIONS ARE
NOT OPTIONAL

Perhaps you can see why it is astonishing to me that so many people try to define true Christianity in terms of decisions and not affections. Not that decisions are unessential. The problem is that they require so little transformation. Mere decisions are no sure evidence of a true work of grace in the heart. People can make "decisions" about the truth of God while their hearts are far from Him.

We have moved far away from the biblical Christianity of Jonathan Edwards. He pointed to 1 Peter 1:8 and argued that "true religion, in great part, consists in the affections."[18]

> Though you have not seen Him, you love Him, and though you do not see Him now, but believe

in Him, you greatly rejoice with joy inexpressible
and full of glory. (1 Peter 1:8)

Throughout Scripture we are commanded to feel, not
just to think or decide. We are commanded to experience
dozens of emotions, not just to perform acts of willpower.

For example, God commands us not to covet (Exodus
20:17), and it is obvious that every commandment not to
have a certain feeling is also a commandment to have a certain feeling. The opposite of covetousness is contentment,
and this is exactly what we are commanded to experience
in Hebrews 13:5: "Be content with what you have" (RSV).

God commands us to bear no grudge (Leviticus 19:18).
The positive side of not bearing a grudge is forgiving "from
the heart." This is what Jesus commands us to do in
Matthew 18:35: "Forgive [your] brother from your heart."
The Bible does not say, Make a mere
decision to drop the grievance. It says,
Experience a change in the heart. The
Bible goes even further and com-
mands a certain intensity. For ex-
ample, 1 Peter 1:22 commands "Love
one another *earnestly* from the heart"
(RSV). And Romans 12:10 commands
"Love one another *with brotherly
affection*" (RSV).

*Being satisfied
in God
is our calling
and duty.*

People are often troubled by the teaching of Christian Hedonism that emotions are part of our duty—that they are commanded. This seems strange partly because emotions are not under our immediate control like acts of willpower seem to be. But Christian Hedonism says, "Consider the Scriptures." Emotions are commanded throughout the Bible.

The Scriptures command joy, hope, fear, peace, grief, desire, tenderheartedness, brokenness and contrition, gratitude, lowliness, etc.[19] Therefore Christian Hedonism is not making too much of emotion when it says that being satisfied in God is our calling and duty.

It is true that our hearts are often sluggish. We do not feel the depth or intensity of affections that are appropriate for God or His cause. It is true that at those times we must exert our wills and make decisions that we hope will rekindle our joy. Even though joyless love is not our aim ("God loves a cheerful giver!" 2 Corinthians 9:7; "[Show] mercy with cheerfulness," Romans 12:8), nevertheless it is better to do a joyless duty than not to do it, provided that there is a spirit of repentance that we have not done all of our duty because of the sluggishness of our hearts.

I am often asked what a Christian should do if the cheerfulness of obedience is not there. It's a good question. My answer is not to simply get on with your duty because feelings don't matter. They do! My answer has three steps. First, confess the sin of joylessness. ("My heart is faint; lead me to the rock that is higher than I," Psalm 61:2.) Acknowledge the coldness of your heart. Don't say that it doesn't matter how you feel. Second, pray earnestly that God would restore the joy of obedience. ("I delight to do Your will, O my God; Your Law is within my heart," Psalm 40:8.) Third, go ahead and do the outward dimension of your duty in the hope that the doing will rekindle the delight.

This is very different from saying: "Do your duty because feelings don't count." These steps assume that there is such a thing as hypocrisy. They are based on the belief that our goal is the reunion of pleasure and duty and that a justification of their separation is a justification of sin.

Yes, it becomes increasingly evident that the experience of joy in God is beyond what the sinful heart can do. It goes against our nature. We are enslaved to pleasure in other things (Romans 6:17). We can't just decide to be glad about something we find boring or uninteresting or offensive—like God. The making of a

The making of a Christian Hedonist is a miracle of sovereign grace.

Christian Hedonist is a miracle of sovereign grace. This is why Paul said that becoming a Christian is the same as being raised from the dead ("even when we were dead in our transgressions, [God] made us alive together with Christ," Ephesians 2:5). It's why Jesus said it was easier for a camel to go through the eye of a needle than for a rich man to stop loving his money and start loving God (Mark 10:25). Camels *can't* go through needles' eyes—just as dead men can't wake themselves from the dead. So Jesus adds, "With people it is impossible, but not with God; for all things are possible with God" (Mark 10:27). So Christian Hedonism breeds an utter dependence on the sovereignty of God. It teaches us to hear the command, "Delight yourself in the LORD," and then to pray with Saint Augustine, "Command what you wish, but give what you command."[20]

Chapter 4

PURSUING PLEASURE
UNDERMINES PRIDE
AND SELF-PITY

Over against all human pride, "God chose what is low and despised in the world…so that no human being might boast in the presence of God" (1 Corinthians 1:28–29, RSV). Any view of the Christian life that claims biblical sanction must be the enemy of pride. This is one of the great values of Christian Hedonism. It undermines the power of pride.

Pride is the primal evil in the universe. The Lord leaves no doubt about how He feels about it: "Pride and arrogance…I hate" (Proverbs 8:13).

Christian Hedonism combats pride because it puts man in the category of an empty vessel beneath the fountain of God. Philanthropists can boast. Welfare recipients can't. The primary experience of the Christian Hedonist is one of helplessness and desperation and longing. When a helpless child is being swept off his feet by the undercurrent on the beach and his father sweeps him up just in time, he does not boast; he hugs.

The nature and depth of human pride are illuminated by comparing boasting to self-pity. Both are manifestations of pride. Boasting is the response of pride to success. Self-pity is the response of pride to suffering. Boasting says, "I deserve admiration because I have achieved so much." Self-pity says, "I deserve admiration because I have suffered so much." Boasting is the voice of pride in the heart of the strong. Self-pity is the voice of pride in the heart of the weak. Boasting sounds self-sufficient. Self-pity sounds self-sacrificing.

The reason self-pity does not look like pride is that it appears to be so needy. But the need arises from a wounded ego. It doesn't come from a sense of unworthiness, but from a sense of unrecognized worthiness. It is the response of unapplauded pride.

Christian Hedonism severs the root of self-pity. People don't feel self-pity when suffering is accepted for the sake of joy.

"Blessed are you when men revile you and persecute you and utter all kinds of evil against you falsely on my account. Rejoice and be glad, for your reward is great in heaven, for so men persecuted the prophets who were before you." (Matthew 5:11–12, RSV)

This is the ax laid to the root of self-pity. When Christian Hedonists have to suffer on account of Christ, they do not summon up their own resources like heroes. They become like little children who trust the strength of their father and who want the joy of his reward. The greatest sufferers for Christ have always deflected praise and pity by testifying to their Christian Hedonism. We will see this especially in the lives of missionaries in the final chapter.

You can see the principle at work among the godly again and again. For example, I knew a seminary professor who also served as an usher in the balcony of a big church. Once when he was to take part in a service, the pastor extolled him for his willingness to serve in this unglamorous role even though he

Christian Hedonism combats pride because it puts man in the category of an empty vessel beneath the fountain of God.

had a doctorate in theology. The professor humbly deflected and softened the praise by quoting Psalm 84:10 (NIV):

> Better is one day in your courts than a thousand elsewhere; I would rather be a doorkeeper in the house of my God than dwell in the tents of the wicked.

In other words, "Don't think that I am heroically overcoming great obstacles of disinclination to keep the doors of the sanctuary. The Word of God says it will bring great blessing! I am maximizing my joy in God." We don't pity or excessively praise those who are simply doing what will make them the most happy. And even when we see this very thing as a virtue, our admiration will be deflected onto the Treasure that satisfies their souls, not the simple experience of satisfaction. Enjoying the infinitely Enjoyable is no great feat. Unless you are spiritually dead. But then the solution is resurrection, and only God raises the dead. What's left for us to do is breathe the sweet air of grace outside the tomb.

We don't pity or excessively praise those who are simply doing what will make them the most happy.

Most people recognize that doing something for joy—
even on the merely horizontal level—is a humbling experience. For example, a businessman may take some friends
out for dinner. When he picks up the check, his friends
begin to say how good it was of him to pay for them. But
he simply lifts his hand in a gesture that says, "Stop." Then
he says, "It's my pleasure." In other words, if I do a good
deed for the joy of it, the impulse of pride is broken. The
breaking of that impulse is the will of God and is one of the
reasons Christian Hedonism is so vital for the Christian life.

Chapter 5

PURSUE YOUR JOY
IN THE JOY
OF THE BELOVED

I hope it is plain so far that if you come to God dutifully, offering Him the reward of your fellowship instead of thirsting after the reward of His, then you exalt yourself above God as His benefactor and belittle Him as a needy beneficiary. That is evil.

The only way to glorify the all-sufficiency of God is to come to Him because in His presence is fullness of joy and at His right hand are pleasures for evermore (Psalm 16:11). We could call this vertical Christian Hedonism. Between man and God, on the vertical axis of life, the pursuit of pleasure is not just tolerable; it is mandatory—"Delight yourself in the LORD!" The chief end of man is to glorify God *by* enjoying Him forever.

But what about horizontal Christian Hedonism? What about relationships of love with other people? Is disinterested benevolence the ideal among men? Or is the pursuit of pleasure proper and indeed mandatory for every kind of human love that pleases God?

Christian Hedonism answers: *The pursuit of pleasure is an essential motive for every good deed. If you aim to abandon the pursuit of full and lasting pleasure, you cannot love people or please God.*

When I preached on this once, a philosophy professor wrote a letter to me with the following criticism:

> Is it not the contention of morality that we should do the good because it is the good?... We should do the good and perform virtuously, I suggest, because it is good and virtuous; that God will bless it and cause us to be happy is a consequence of it, but not the motive for doing it.

Another popular writer says, "For the Christian, happiness is never a goal to be pursued. It is always the unexpected surprise of a life of service."

These quotes represent the flood of common opinion

that a Christian Hedonist swims against all the time. He regards them as contrary to Scripture and contrary to love and, in the end, dishonoring to God.

No doubt, biblical passages come to mind that seem to say exactly the opposite of what Christian Hedonism is saying. For example, in the great "love chapter" the apostle Paul says that love "does not seek its own" (1 Corinthians 13:5). Does this mean that it would be unloving to delight in doing good?

According to the prophet Micah, God has commanded us not simply to be kind, but to love kindness. "He has told you, O man, what is good; and what does the LORD require of you but to do justice, to love kindness, and to walk humbly with your God?" (Micah 6:8). Does obedience to the command to "love kindness" mean you must disobey the teaching of 1 Corinthians 13:5 that love should not "seek its own" when you show mercy?

No. That is not what Paul is thinking. We know it isn't, because in verse 3 he actually motivates love by our longing for gain: "If I give away all I have, and if I deliver my body to be burned, but have not love, *I gain nothing*" (RSV). If genuine love dare not set its sights on its own gain, isn't it strange that Paul should warn us that not having love will rob us of "gain"?

Giving Paul the benefit of the doubt, should we not

assume there is a kind of "gain" that is wrong to be motivated by (hence "Love seeks not its own") and that there is also a kind of "gain" that is right to be motivated by (hence "If I do not have love, I gain nothing")? What is this proper gain? Jonathan Edwards gives a compelling answer:

> In some sense the most benevolent, generous person in the world seeks his own happiness in doing good to others, because he places his happiness in their good. His mind is so enlarged as to take them, as it were, into himself. Thus when they are happy, he feels it; he partakes with them, and is happy in their happiness.[21]

In other words, when Paul says, "Love seeks not its own," he does not mean that love may not rejoice in loving. Rather he means that love will not seek its own private comforts and ease at the expense of others.

The moral value of an act of love is not ruined when we are motivated to do it by the anticipation of our own joy in it and from it. If it were, then a bad man, who hated the prospect of loving, could engage in pure love since he would take no joy in it; while a good man, who delighted in the prospect of loving, could not love since he would "gain" joy from it and thus ruin it.

Therefore, 1 Corinthians 13:5 ("Love seeks not its

own") does not stand in the way of Christian Hedonism. On the contrary, taken together with 1 Corinthians 13:3 ("If I deliver my body to be burned, but have not love, I gain nothing"), it supports and clarifies Christian Hedonism: *The pursuit of true gain is an essential motive for every good deed.*

What is this "true gain"? In 2 Corinthians 8 Paul shows that genuine love always relates to *God* as gain. The situation is that the churches in Macedonia have demonstrated what true love is by the way they responded in generosity to Paul's appeal for the poor in Jerusalem. Now he explains to the Corinthians what the nature of this love is.

> We wish to make known to you the grace of God which has been given in the churches of Macedonia, that in a great ordeal of affliction their abundance of joy and their deep poverty overflowed in the wealth of their liberality. For I testify that according to their ability, and beyond their ability, they gave of their own accord, begging us with much urging for the favor of participation in the support of the saints. (2 Corinthians 8:1–4)

We know this is a description of love because in verse 8 Paul says, "I say...to prove by the earnestness of others that your *love also* is genuine" (RSV). So here we have a test case to see just what the love of 1 Corinthians 13 looks like in real life. The Macedonians have given away their possessions just as 1 Corinthians 13:3 says ("If I give away all I have"). But *here* it is real love, while *there* it was not love at all. What makes the Macedonian generosity a genuine act of love?

The nature of genuine love can be seen in four things:

- First, it's a work of divine grace. "We wish to make known to you the grace of God which has been given in the churches of Macedonia" (2 Corinthians 8:1). The generosity of the Macedonians was not of human origin. It was a work of grace in their hearts.
- Second, this experience of God's grace filled the Macedonians with joy. "In a great ordeal of affliction their abundance of joy and their deep poverty over-flowed in the wealth of their liberality" (2 Corinthians 8:2). Their joy was not owing to the fact that God had prospered them financially. He hadn't! In extreme poverty they had joy. Therefore the joy was a joy in God, not things.
- Third, their joy in God's grace overflowed in generosity to meet the needs of others. "Their abundance of joy and their deep poverty overflowed in the wealth of their liberality" (2 Corinthians 8:2).

Therefore the liberality expressed horizontally toward men was an overflow of joy in God's grace.

- Fourth, the Macedonians begged for the opportunity to sacrifice their meager possessions for the saints in Jerusalem. "Beyond their ability, they gave of their own accord, begging us with much urging for the favor of participation in the support of the saints" (2 Corinthians 8:3–4). In other words, the way their joy in God overflowed was in the joy of giving. They wanted to give. It was their joy!

Now we can give a definition of love that takes God into account and also includes the feelings that should accompany the outward acts of love: *Love is the overflow and expansion of joy in God, which gladly meets the needs of others.* Love is not merely the passive overflow, but the aggressive extension and expansion and completion of joy in God, reaching even to the poor in Jerusalem.

Love is the overflow and expansion of joy in God, which gladly meets the needs of others.

This is why a person can give his body to be burned and not have love (1 Corinthians 13:3). Love is the overflow and expansion of joy *in God!* It is not duty for duty's sake, or right for right's sake. It is not a resolute abandoning of one's own good with a view solely to the good of the other person. It is first a deeply satisfying experience of the fullness of God's grace, and then a doubly satisfying experience of extending this joy in God to another person.

The Macedonians discovered the labor of Christian Hedonism: Love! It is the overflow and expansion of joy in God, which gladly meets the needs of others.

I hope it is becoming clear why I say: If you try to abandon the pursuit of your full and lasting joy, you cannot love people or please God. If love is the overflow and expansion of joy in God which gladly meets the needs of others, then to abandon the pursuit of this joy is to abandon the pursuit of love! And if God is pleased by cheerful givers, then to abandon the pursuit of this cheerfulness sets you on a course in which God takes no delight. If we are indifferent about whether we do a good deed cheerfully, we are indifferent to what pleases God.

Therefore it is essential that we be Christian Hedonists on the horizontal level in our relationships with other people and not just on the vertical axis in our relationship with God. If love is the overflow and expansion of joy in God that gladly meets the needs of other people, and if God loves such joyful givers, then this joy in giving is a Christian duty, and not pursuing it is sin.

It would be easy to misunderstand Christian Hedonism at this point as if there were no weeping in it, because the stress on joy may seem to rule out pain and sorrow. This would be a great mistake. Paul describes his life with the phrase, "sorrowful yet always rejoicing" (2 Corinthians 6:10). He commands us to "weep with those who weep" (Romans 12:15). When he thinks about his perishing kinsmen he says, "I have great sorrow and unceasing grief in my heart" (Romans 9:2). When he writes to churches in sin it is "out of much affliction and anguish of heart…and with many tears" (2 Corinthians 2:4).

The contentment of a Christian Hedonist is not mystical serenity, unmoved by the hurts of others. In this fallen age of futility it is a profoundly dissatisfied contentment. It is constantly hungry for more of the feast of God's grace. And even the measure of contentment that God grants here and now contains an insatiable impulse to expand itself to others (2 Corinthians 8:4; 1 John 1:4).

Christian joy reveals itself as dissatisfied contentment whenever it perceives human need. It starts to expand in love to fill that need and bring about the joy of faith in the heart of the other person. But since there is often an obstacle, or a time lapse, between our perception of a person's need and our eventual rejoicing in the person's restored joy, there is a place for weeping in that interval. The weeping of compassion is the weeping of joy impeded in the extension of itself to another.

If we took no pleasure in the good of others, we would feel no pain when the good is impeded. So make no mistake, love is on a passionate pursuit to satisfy our deepest longings in the God-centered good of the beloved. Christian Hedonism rejects the high sounding philosophy that says, "For the Christian, happiness is never a goal to be pursued. It is always the unexpected surprise of a life of service."

One of the clearest biblical reasons for rejecting this common view is Paul's quotation of the words of Jesus in Acts 20:35. There are many tears as Paul finishes his farewell address to the Ephesian elders. He says, "In everything I showed you that by working hard in this manner you must help the weak and remember the words of the Lord Jesus, that He Himself said, 'It is more blessed to give than to receive.'"

We will not feel the hedonistic force of these words if we do not meditate on the word *remember*. Paul did not just say that it is more blessed to give than to receive. He said that it is crucial in our labors of love to *remember* this. Keep it in mind. Don't forget it. Let it have its motivating effect.

Most Christians today agree that it is more blessed to

give than to receive. But many have serious doubts that we should be *motivated* by this truth. They say that blessing comes as a *result* of giving, but that if you keep this fact before you as a motive, it will ruin the moral value of your giving and turn you into a mercenary. The word *remember* in Acts 20:35 is a great obstacle to this popular wisdom. Why would Paul tell church elders to *keep in mind* the joyful blessings of giving if in fact doing so would turn ministers into mercenaries?

I do not see how anyone can honor the word *remember* in Acts 20:35 and still think it is wrong to pursue the reward of joy in the ministry. On the contrary, Paul thinks it is necessary to keep the joy set firmly before us. *"Remember!* It is more blessed to give than to receive."

One reason Paul spoke this way is that the cost of love is so high in this life we could never survive it without the hope of Christ-centered joy in this life and beyond the grave. Paul said, "If we have hoped in Christ in this life only, we are of all men most to be pitied" (1 Corinthians 15:19). In other words, a life of love, with all the pain and risk involved, would be a fool's life if there were no recompense beyond the grave.

He was following his Master in this mindset because Jesus motivated hard acts of love in the same way: "You will be blessed [when you serve the poor], since they do not have the means to repay you; for you will be repaid at the resurrection of the righteous" (Luke 14:14).

Love is costly. It always involves some kind of self-denial in this world. "He who loves his life loses it, and he who hates his life *in this world* will keep it to life eternal" (John 12:25). Love costs you your life in this world. But in the world to come the joys of eternal life are more than sufficient reward. Christian Hedonism insists that the eternal gain outweighs temporary pain. It affirms that there are rare and wonderful species of joy that flourish only in the rainy atmosphere of suffering. "The soul would have no rainbow if the eye had no tears."[22]

The writer of the book of Hebrews taught this with relentless clarity.

Where does compassion on prisoners come from when the cost may be the seizure of your property? Here is the answer from the first century church: "You showed sympathy to the prisoners and accepted *joyfully* the seizure of your property, knowing that you have for yourselves a better possession and a lasting one" (Hebrews 10:34).

In the early days of their conversion, some Christians had been imprisoned for their faith. The others were confronted with a difficult choice: Shall we go underground and stay "safe," or shall we visit our brothers and sisters in prison and risk our lives and our property? They chose the way of love and accepted the risk. "You showed sympathy to the prisoners and accepted *joyfully* the seizure of your property." The key to love was joy.

But where did this joy come from? Answer: "Knowing that you have for yourselves a better possession and a lasting one." This word *knowing* functions just like the word *remember* in Acts 20:35— *"Remember* the words of the Lord Jesus, that He Himself said, 'It is more blessed to give than to receive.'" It was *knowing* that God offered them a *better* and *lasting* reward that freed the Christians to risk the cost of love.

The power to love was sustained by the pursuit of better and lasting joy.

Again the writer drives the same point home with the example of Moses in Hebrews 11.

> By faith Moses, when he had grown up, refused to be called the son of Pharaoh's daughter, choosing rather to endure ill-treatment with the people of God than to enjoy the passing pleasures of sin, considering the reproach of Christ greater riches than the treasures of Egypt; for he was looking to the reward. (verses 24–26)

Moses is a hero for the church because his joy in the promised reward caused him to count the pleasures of Egypt as rubbish by comparison. They were too short and too small, compared to the reward. This pursuit of the full and lasting reward of Christ-centered joy bound Moses forever to Israel in love. He endured incredible hardship in the service of God's people when he could have had a lifetime of comforts in Egypt. The power of love was the pursuit of the greater pleasures in the presence of God over the fleeting pleasures of sin in Egypt.

But the writer of Hebrews has saved the most amazing example for last. What sustained the greatest act of love that has ever been performed in the history of the world—the agonizing death of Jesus in our place? The answer is the same: "[Fix your] eyes on Jesus, the author and perfecter of faith, who *for the joy set before Him* endured the cross" (Hebrews 12:2).

The greatest labor of love that ever happened was possible because Jesus pursued the greatest imaginable joy, namely, the joy of being exalted to God's right hand in the assembly of a redeemed people. For the joy that was set before Him, He endured the cross!

Christian Hedonism is utterly committed to loving like Jesus. We do not presume to live by motives greater than the ones He lived by. What hinders love in the world today? Is it that we are all trying to please ourselves? *No!* It is because we are all too easily pleased.

The message that needs to be shouted from the

Quit being satisfied with little 2-percent yields of pleasure that get eaten up by the moths of inflation and the rust of death.

housetops is: Listen, world! You are not nearly hedonistic enough! You are far too easily pleased. You are like children making mud pies in the slum because you cannot imagine what a holiday at the sea is like. Stop laying up for yourselves treasures on earth where moth and rust consume and where thieves break in and steal. Lay up for yourselves treasures in heaven! (Matthew 6:19–20).

Quit being satisfied with little 2-percent yields of pleasure that get eaten up by the moths of inflation and the rust of death. Invest in the blue-chip, high-yield, divinely insured securities of heaven. Giving your life to material comforts and thrills is like throwing money down a rat hole. But a life invested in the labor of love yields dividends of joy unsurpassed and unending—even if it costs you your property and your life on this earth.

Come to Christ in whose presence are fullness of joy and pleasures forever more. Join the labor of Christian Hedonism. For the Lord of heaven and earth, Jesus Christ, has spoken: It is more blessed to love than to live in luxury!

So far we have seen a brief sketch of the way of life I call Christian Hedonism. I have tried to give a glimpse of what it means vertically in relation to God and horizontally in relation to man—that it is essential for all true worship and virtue. It glorifies God, it undermines pride, it captures the affections of the heart, and it carries the cost of love. I have tried to show that it is thoroughly biblical and old fashioned, yet radical and controversial.

Now I turn to illustrate some practical effects of this vision in four areas of life and ministry: corporate worship, marriage, money, and missions. If the vision is true, the fruit in all these areas should be the glory of God and the holiness of His people.

Chapter 6

WHAT DOES IT
MEAN FOR WORSHIP?

The modern revolt against old-fashioned Christian Hedonism has killed the spirit of worship in many churches and many hearts. The widespread notion that high moral acts must be free from self-interest is a great enemy of true worship. Worship is the highest moral act a human can perform; so the only basis and motivation for it that many people can conceive is the moral notion of disinterested performance of duty. But when worship is reduced to disinterested duty, it ceases to be worship. For worship is a feast of the glorious perfections of God in Christ.

God is not honored when we celebrate the high days of our relationship out of a mere sense of duty. He is honored when those days are our delight! Therefore to honor God in worship we must not seek Him disinterestedly, for fear of gaining some joy in worship and so ruining the moral value of the act. Instead, we must seek Him hedonistically, the way a thirsty deer pants after the stream, precisely for the joy of seeing and savoring God! Worship is nothing less than obedience to the command of God, "Delight yourself in the LORD" (Psalm 37:4).

Misguided virtue smothers the spirit of worship. The person who has the vague notion that it is a virtue to overcome self-interest and that it is a vice to seek pleasure will scarcely be able to worship. For worship is the most hedonistic affair of life and must not be ruined with the least thought of disinterestedness. The great hindrance to worship is not that we are a pleasure-seeking people, but that we are willing to settle for such pitiful pleasures.

The great hindrance to worship is not that we are a pleasure-seeking people, but that we are willing to settle for such pitiful pleasures.

Every Sunday at 11 A.M., Hebrews 11:6 enters combat with popular conceptions of selfless virtue. "And without faith it is impossible to please Him, for he who comes to God must believe that *He is and that He is a rewarder of those who seek Him.*" You cannot please God if you do not come to Him for reward! Therefore, worship that pleases God is the hedonistic pursuit of God. He is our exceedingly great reward! In His presence is fullness of joy, and at His right hand are *pleasures* forevermore. Being satisfied with all God is for us in Jesus is the essence of the authentic experience of worship. Worship is the feast of Christian Hedonism.

Consider three implications for corporate worship.

First, the true diagnosis of weak worship is *not* that our people are coming to get and not to give. Not a few pastors scold their people that the worship services would be lively if people came to give instead of to get. There is a better diagnosis.

People *ought* to come to corporate worship services to get. They ought to come starved for God. They ought to come saying, "As the deer pants for the water brooks, so my soul pants for You, O God" (Psalm 42:1). God is profoundly honored when people know that they will die of hunger and thirst unless they have God. And it is my job as a preacher to spread a banquet for them. I must show them from Scripture what they are really starving for—God—and then feed them well until they say, "Ahhh." That is worship.

Second, seeing the essence of worship as satisfaction in God will make corporate worship radically God-centered.

Nothing makes God more supreme and more central than when people are utterly persuaded that nothing—not money or prestige or leisure or family or job or health or sports or toys or friends—is going to bring satisfaction to their aching hearts besides God. This conviction breeds people who go hard after God on Sunday morning.

If the focus shifts onto our giving to God, instead of His giving Himself to us, one result is that subtly it is not God who remains at the center but, instead, the quality of our giving. Are we singing worthily of the Lord? Are our instrumentalists playing with quality fitting a gift to the Lord? Is the preaching a suitable offering to the Lord? This all sounds noble at first. But little by little the focus shifts off the utter indispensability of the Lord Himself and onto the quality of our performances. And we even start to define excellence and power in worship in terms of the technical distinction of our artistic acts.

Nothing keeps God at the center of worship like the biblical conviction that the essence of worship is deep, heartfelt satisfaction in Him and the conviction that the pursuit of that satisfaction is why we are together.

Third, Christian Hedonism protects the primacy of worship by forcing us to see that the essential heart-act of worship as an end in itself.

If the essence of worship is satisfaction in God, then

worship can't be a means to anything else. You simply can't say to God, "I want to be satisfied in You so that I can have something else." Because that would mean that you are not really satisfied in God but in that something else. And that would dishonor God, not worship Him.

If the essence of worship is satisfaction in God, then worship can't be a means to anything else.

But in fact, for many people and pastors, the event of "worship" on Sunday morning is conceived of as a means to accomplish something other than worship. We "worship" to raise money; we "worship" to attract crowds; we "worship" to heal human hurts; we "worship" to recruit workers; we "worship" to improve church morale; we "worship" to give talented musicians an opportunity to fulfill their calling; we "worship" to teach our children the way of righteousness; we "worship" to help marriages stay together; we "worship" to evangelize the lost among us; we "worship" to give our churches a family feeling, etc., etc.

In all of this we belittle worship and God. Genuine affections for God are an end in themselves. I cannot say to my wife: "I feel a strong delight in you—so that you will make me a nice meal." That is not the way delight works.

It terminates on her. It does not have a nice meal in view. I cannot say to my son, "I love playing ball with you—so that you will cut the grass." If your heart really delights in playing with him, that delight cannot be performed as a means to getting him to do something.

I am not denying that vital corporate worship might have a hundred good effects on the life of the church. It will, like true affection in marriage, make everything better. My point is that to the degree that we "worship" for these reasons, it ceases to be authentic worship. Keeping satisfaction in God at the center guards us from that tragedy.

Chapter 7

WHAT DOES IT MEAN FOR MARRIAGE?

The reason there is so much misery in marriage is not that husbands and wives seek their own pleasure, but that they do not seek it in the pleasure of their spouses. The biblical mandate to husbands and wives is to seek your own joy in the joy of your spouse. Make marriage a matrix for Christian Hedonism.

There is scarcely a more hedonistic passage in the Bible than the one on marriage in Ephesians 5:25–30.

> Husbands, love your wives, just as Christ also loved the church and gave Himself up for her, so that He might sanctify her, having cleansed her by

the washing of water with the word, that He might present to Himself the church in all her glory, having no spot or wrinkle or any such thing; but that she would be holy and blameless. So husbands ought also to love their own wives as their own bodies. He who loves his own wife loves himself; for no one ever hated his own flesh, but nourishes and cherishes it, just as Christ also does the church, because we are members of His body.

Husbands are told to love their wives the way Christ loved the church. How did He love the church? "He gave Himself up for her." But why? "That He might sanctify and cleanse her." But why did He want to do that? "That He might present to Himself the church in all her glory."

Ah! There it is! "For the joy that was set before Him, [He] endured the cross" (Hebrews 12:2). What joy? The joy of marriage to His bride, the church. Jesus does not want a dirty and unholy wife. Therefore He was willing to die to "sanctify and cleanse" His betrothed so He could present to Himself a wife "in all her glory."

The biblical mandate to husbands and wives is to seek your own joy in the joy of your spouse.

And what is the church's ultimate joy? Is it not to be cleansed and sanctified and then presented as a bride to the sovereign, all-glorious Christ? So Christ sought His own joy, yes—but He sought it in the joy of the church! That is what love does: It pursues its own joy in the joy of the beloved.

In Ephesians 5:29–30, Paul pushes the hedonism of Christ even further: "For no one ever hated his own flesh, but nourishes and cherishes it, just as Christ also does the church, because we are members of His body." Why does Christ nourish and cherish the church? Because we are members of His own body, and no man ever hates his own body. In other words, the union between Christ and His bride is so close ("one flesh") that any good done to her is a good done to Himself. The blatant assertion of this text is that this fact motivates the Lord to nourish, cherish, sanctify, and cleanse His bride.

By some popular definitions this cannot be love. Love, they say, must be free of self-interest—especially Christlike love, especially Calvary love. I have never seen such a view of love made to square with this passage of Scripture. What Christ does for His bride this text plainly calls love. "Husbands, love your wives, just as Christ also loved the church." Why not let the text define love for us, instead of bringing our definition from ethics or philosophy?

According to this text, love is the pursuit of our joy in the holy joy of the beloved. There is no way to exclude self-interest from love, but self-interest is not the same as selfishness. Selfishness seeks its own private happiness at the expense of others. Love seeks its happiness *in* the happiness of the beloved. It will even suffer and die for the beloved in order that its joy might be full in the life and purity of the beloved.

For a husband to be an obedient person he must love his wife the way Christ loved the church. That is, he must pursue his own joy in the holy joy of his wife. "So husbands ought also to love their own wives as their own bodies. He who loves his own wife loves himself" (verse 28). In other words, husbands should devote the same energy and time and creativity to making their wives happy that they devote naturally to making themselves happy. The result will be that in doing this they will make themselves happy. For he who loves his wife loves himself. Since the wife is one flesh with her husband, the same applies to her love for him.

Paul does not build a dam against

Put the glory of Christ on display by pursuing your joy in the holy joy of your beloved.

the river of hedonism; he builds a channel for it. He says, "Husbands and wives, recognize that in marriage you have become one flesh. If you live for your private pleasure at the expense of your spouse, you are living against yourself and destroying your joy. But if you devote yourself with all your heart to the holy joy of your spouse, you will also be living for your joy and making a marriage after the image of Christ and His church." This is what God intended for marriage: Put the glory of Christ on display by pursuing your joy in the holy joy of your beloved.

Chapter 8

WHAT DOES IT
MEAN FOR
MONEY?

Money is the currency of Christian Hedonism. What you do with it—or desire to do with it—can make or break your happiness forever. The Bible makes clear that what you feel about money can destroy you: "Those who want to get rich fall into temptation and a snare and many foolish and harmful desires which plunge men into ruin and destruction" (1 Timothy 6:9).

This passage teaches us to use our money in a way that will bring us the greatest and longest gain. That is, it advocates Christian Hedonism. It confirms that it is not only permitted but also commanded by God that we flee from destruction and pursue our full and lasting pleasure. It implies that all the evils in the world come not because our desires for happiness are too strong, but because they are so weak that we settle for fleeting, money-bought pleasures that do not satisfy our deepest longings, but in the end destroy our souls. The root of all evil is that we are the kind of people who settle for the love of money instead of the love of God (1 Timothy 6:10).

1 Timothy 6:5–10 is so crucial that we should meditate on it in more detail. Paul is warning Timothy against those:

> …who suppose that godliness is a means of gain. But godliness actually is a means of great gain when accompanied by contentment. For we have brought nothing into the world, so we cannot take anything out of it either. If we have food and covering, with these we shall be content. But those who want to get rich fall into temptation and a snare and many foolish and harmful desires which plunge men into ruin and destruction. For the love of money is a root of all sorts of evil, and some by longing for it have wandered away from the faith and pierced themselves with many griefs.

In other words, watch out for slick deceivers who have discovered that they can cash in on an upsurge of godliness. According to verse 5, these folks treat godliness as a means of gain. They are so addicted to money that truth has a very small place in their affections. They don't "rejoice in the truth." They rejoice in tax evasion. They are willing to use any new, popular interest to make a few bucks. If the bottom line is big and black, misleading advertising strategies don't matter. If godliness is in, then sell godliness.

Paul could have responded to this effort to turn godliness into gain by saying, "Christians do what's right for its own sake. Christians aren't motivated by profit." But that's *not* what Paul said. He said, "Godliness actually is a means of great gain when accompanied by contentment" (verse 6). Instead of saying Christians don't live for gain, he says that Christians ought to live for *greater* gain than the slick money lovers do. Godliness is the way to get this great gain, but only if we are content with simplicity rather than greedy for riches. "Godliness *with contentment* is great gain."

If your godliness has freed you from the desire to be rich and has helped you be content with what you have, then your godliness is tremendously profitable. "For bodily discipline is only of little profit, but godliness is profitable for all things, since it holds promise for the present life and also for the life to come" (1 Timothy 4:8). Godliness that overcomes the craving for material wealth produces great spiritual wealth. The point of verse 6 is that it is very profitable not to pursue wealth.

What follows in verses 7–10 are three reasons we should not pursue riches.

But first let me insert a clarification. Many legitimate businesses depend on large concentrations of capital. You can't build a new manufacturing plant (which employs thousands of people and makes a worthwhile commodity) without millions of dollars in equity. Therefore, financial officers often have the responsibility to build reserves.

When the Bible condemns the desire to get rich, it is not necessarily condemning a business that aims to expand and therefore seeks larger capital reserves. The officers of the business might be greedy for more personal wealth, or they may have larger, nobler motives of how their expanded productivity will benefit people.

Even when a competent businessperson accepts a raise or a higher-paying job, that is not enough to condemn him for the desire to be rich. He might have accepted the job because he craves power and status and luxuries. Or, content with what he has, he may intend to use the extra money for founding an adoption agency or giving scholarships or sending missionaries or funding an inner-city ministry.

Working to earn money for the cause of Christ is not the same as desiring to be rich. What Paul is warning against is not the desire to earn money to meet our needs and the needs of others; he is warning against the desire to *have* more and more money with the ego boost and material luxuries it can provide.

Let's look at the three reasons Paul gives in verses 7–10 for why we should not aspire to be rich.

First, in verse 7 he says, "We have brought nothing into the world, so we cannot take anything out of it either." There are no U-Hauls behind hearses.

The person who spends himself to get rich in this life is a fool. He is out of touch with reality. We will go out just the way we came in. Picture hundreds of people entering eternity in a plane crash in the Sea of Japan. They stand before God utterly stripped of Visa cards, checkbooks, credit lines, image clothes, how-to-succeed books, and Hilton reservations. Here are the politician, the executive, the playboy, and the missionary kid, all on level ground with absolutely nothing in their hands, possessing only what they brought in their hearts. How absurd and tragic the lover of money will seem on that day.

Don't spend your precious life trying to get rich, Paul says, "For we have brought nothing into the world, so we cannot take anything out of it either."

Second, in verse 8 Paul adds another reason not to pursue wealth: "If we have food and covering, with these we shall be content." Christians can be and ought to be content with the necessities of life. When you have God near you and for you, you don't need extra money or extra things to give you peace and security. Hebrews 13:5–6 makes this crystal clear:

> Make sure that your character is free from the love of money, being content with what you have; for He Himself has said, "I WILL NEVER DESERT YOU, NOR WILL I EVER FORSAKE YOU," so that we confidently say, "THE LORD IS MY HELPER, I WILL NOT BE AFRAID. WHAT WILL MAN DO TO ME?"

No matter which way the market is moving, God is always better than gold. His promises of help sever the cords of bondage to the love of money.

The third reason not to pursue wealth is that the pursuit will end in the destruction of your life. This is the point of verses 9–10:

> But those who want to get rich fall into temptation and a snare and many foolish and harmful desires which plunge men into ruin and destruction. For the love of money is a root of all sorts of evil, and some by longing for it have wandered away from the faith and pierced themselves with many griefs.

No Christian Hedonist wants to plunge into ruin and destruction and be pierced with many griefs. Therefore, no Christian Hedonist desires to be rich. Instead we want to use our money to maximize our joy the way Jesus taught us to. Jesus is not against investment. He is against bad investment—namely, setting our hearts on the comforts and securities that money can afford in this world. Money is to be invested for eternal yields in heaven: "Store up for yourselves treasures in heaven" (Matthew 6:20). How?

Luke 12:32–34 gives one answer:

> "Do not be afraid, little flock, for your Father has chosen gladly to give you the kingdom. Sell your possessions and give to charity; make yourselves money belts which do not wear out, an unfailing treasure in heaven, where no thief comes near nor moth destroys. For where your treasure is, there your heart will be also."

God is not glorified when we keep for ourselves (no matter how thankfully) what we ought to be using to alleviate the misery of unevangelized, uneducated, unmedicated, and unfed millions.

So the answer to how to store up treasure in heaven is to spend your earthly treasures for merciful purposes in Christ's name here on earth. Give to those in need—that is how you provide yourself with money belts in heaven. Notice carefully that Jesus does not merely say that treasure in heaven will be the unexpected result of generosity on earth. No, He says we should pursue treasure in heaven. Store it up! "Make yourselves money belts...an unfailing treasure in heaven!" This is pure Christian Hedonism.

God is not glorified when we keep for ourselves (no matter how thankfully) what we ought to be using to alleviate the misery of unevangelized, uneducated, unmedicated, and unfed millions. The evidence that many professing Christians have been deceived by Western commercialism and materialism is how little we give and how much we own. And by an almost irresistible law of consumerism we have bought bigger (and more) houses, newer (and more) cars, fancier (and more) clothes, better (and more) meat, and all manner of trinkets and gadgets and containers and devices and equipment to make life more fun.

Some Christians may object: Does not the Bible promise that God will prosper His people? Indeed! God increases our yield so that by giving we can prove that our yield is not our god. God does not prosper a man's business so he can move from a Ford to a BMW. God prospers a business so that thousands of unreached peoples can be reached with the gospel. He prospers a business so that 20 percent of the world's population can move a step back from the precipice of starvation.

Life is war. The casualties are millions, and the stakes are eternal. What we need today is not a call to simplicity, but a call to war. We need to think in terms of a "wartime lifestyle" rather than a "simple lifestyle." I have used the phrase "necessities of life" because Paul said in 1 Timothy 6:8, "If we have food and covering, with these we shall be content." But this idea of simple necessity can be misleading. I mean it to refer to a style of life that is unencumbered with nonessentials—and the criterion for "essential" should not be primitive simplicity, but wartime effectiveness.

Missionary visionary Ralph Winter illustrates this idea of a wartime lifestyle:

> The Queen Mary, lying in repose in the harbor at Long Beach, California, is a fascinating museum of the past. Used both as a luxury liner in peacetime and a troop transport during the Second World War, its present status as a museum the length of three football fields affords a stunning contrast between the lifestyles appropriate in peace and war. On one side of a partition you see the dining room reconstructed to depict the peacetime table setting that was appropriate to the wealthy

patrons of high culture for whom a dazzling array of knives and forks and spoons held no mysteries. On the other side of the partition the evidences of wartime austerities are in sharp contrast. One metal tray with indentations replaces fifteen plates and saucers. Bunks, not just double but eight tiers high, explain why the peacetime complement of 3000 gave way to 15,000 people on board in wartime. How repugnant to the peacetime masters this transformation must have been! To do it took a national emergency, of course. The survival of a nation depended upon it. The essence of the Great Commission today is that the survival of many millions of people depends on its fulfillment.[23]

Life is war. All talk of a Christian's right to live luxuriously "as a child of the King" in this atmosphere sounds hollow—especially since the King Himself stripped for battle.

The message of Christian Hedonism rings clear in 1 Timothy 6. It is mainly about money and the aim is to help us lay hold on eternal life. Beware the desire to get rich (verse 9). "Fight the good fight of faith; take hold of the eternal life" (verse 12). Paul never dabbles in nonessentials. He lives on the brink of eternity. That's why he sees things so clearly. You want life "which is life indeed," don't you (verse 19)? You don't want ruin, destruction, and pangs of heart, do you (verses 9–10)? You want all the gain that godliness can bring, don't you (verse 6)?

Then use the currency of Christian Hedonism wisely: Do not desire to be rich; be content with the wartime necessities of life; set your hope fully on God; guard yourself from pride; and let your joy in God overflow in a wealth of liberality to a lost and needy world.

Life is war. All talk of a Christian's right to live luxuriously "as a child of the King" in this atmosphere sounds hollow— especially since the King Himself stripped for battle.

Chapter 9

WHAT DOES IT
MEAN FOR
MISSIONS?

It is clear from what we saw about money that the battle cry of Christian Hedonism is world missions—sacrificing the comforts and securities of home for the unreached peoples of the world. Paradoxically, here where the sacrifices are greatest, the joys are deepest. And the pursuit of these joys is the driving engine of world evangelization.

After Jesus told His disciples that it would be hard for the rich to enter the kingdom of heaven (Mark 10:23), Peter said, "Behold, we have left everything and followed You" (verse 28). Evidently Jesus heard a trace of self-pity. What He said to Peter has caused a thousand missionaries to lay down everything at home to follow Christ to the hardest places of the world. Jesus said:

> "Truly I say to you, there is no one who has left house or brothers or sisters or mother or father or children or farms, for My sake and for the gospel's sake, but that he will receive a hundred times as much now in the present age, houses and brothers and sisters and mothers and children and farms, along with persecutions; and in the age to come, eternal life." (Mark 10:29–30)

This does not mean you get materially rich by becoming a missionary. If you volunteer for mission service with such a notion, the Lord will confront you with these words: "Foxes have holes and the birds of the air have nests, but the Son of Man has nowhere to lay His head" (Luke 9:58).

Instead, the point is that if you are deprived of your earthly family in the service of Christ, it will be made up a hundredfold in your spiritual family, the church. Yes, but what about the solitary missionaries who labor for years without being surrounded by hundreds of sisters and brothers and mothers and children in the faith? Is the promise true for them?

Yes it is. Surely what Christ means is that He Himself makes up for every sacrifice. If you give up a mother's nearby affection and concern, you get it back one hundred times in the affection and concern from the ever-present Christ. If you give up the warm comradeship of a brother, you get back one hundred times the warmth and comradeship of Christ. If you give up the sense of at-homeness you had in your house, you get back one hundred times the comfort and security of knowing that your Lord owns all the houses and lands and streams and trees on earth. To prospective missionaries, Jesus says, I promise to be with you (Matthew 28:20). I will *work* for you and *be* for you so much that you will not be able to speak of having sacrificed anything.

In essence, Jesus says that when you "deny yourself" for His sake and the gospel, you are denying yourself a lesser good for a greater good. In other words, Jesus wants us to think about sacrifice in a way that rules out all self-pity. This is, in fact, just what the texts on self-denial teach.

> "If anyone wishes to come after Me, he must deny himself, and take up his cross and follow Me. For whoever wishes to save his life will lose it, but who-ever loses his life for My sake and the gospel's will save it." (Mark 8:34–35)

Jesus does not ask us to be indifferent to whether we are destroyed. On the contrary, He assumes that the long-ing for true life will move us to deny ourselves all the lesser pleasures and comforts of life. The measure of our longing for life is the amount of comfort we are willing to give up to get it. The gift of eternal life in God's presence is glorified if we are willing to hate our lives in this world in order to lay hold of it (John 12:25). Therein lies the God-centered value of self-denial.

This is why so many missionaries have said, after lives of great sacrifice, "I never made a sacrifice." On December 4, 1857, David Livingstone, the great pioneer missionary to Africa, made a stirring appeal to the students of Cambridge University, showing that he had learned through years of experience what Jesus was trying to teach Peter:

> People talk of the sacrifice I have made in spending so much of my life in Africa.... Away with the word in such a view, and with such a thought! It is emphatically no sacrifice. Say rather it is a privilege. Anxiety, sickness, suffering, or danger, now and then, with a foregoing of the common conveniences and charities of this life, may make us pause, and cause the spirit to waver, and the soul to sink; but let this only be for a moment. All these are nothing when compared with the glory which shall be revealed in and for us [Romans 8:18]. I never made a sacrifice.[24]

The great incentive for throwing our lives into the cause of missions is the 10,000-percent return on the investment. Missionaries have borne witness to this from the beginning—since the apostle Paul.

> But whatever things were gain to me, those things I have counted as loss for the sake of Christ. More than that, I count all things to be loss in view of the surpassing value of knowing Christ Jesus my Lord, for whom I have suffered the loss of all things, and count them but rubbish so that I may gain Christ...that I may know Him and the power of His resurrection and the fellowship of His sufferings, being conformed to His death. (Philippians 3:7–8, 10)

> For momentary, light affliction is producing for us an eternal weight of glory far beyond all comparison. (2 Corinthians 4:17; see Romans 8:18)

It is simply amazing how consistent are the testimonies of missionaries who have suffered for the gospel. Virtually all of them bear witness to the abundant joy and overriding compensations.[25]

Missions is the automatic outflow and overflow of love for Christ. We delight to enlarge our joy in Him by extending it to others. As Lottie Moon said, "Surely there can be no greater joy than that of saving souls."[26]

The great incentive for throwing our lives into the cause of missions is the 10,000-percent return on the investment.

In 1897, Samuel Zwemer and his wife and two daughters sailed to the Persian Gulf to work among the Muslims of Bahrain. Their evangelism was largely fruitless. In July 1904 both the daughters, ages four and seven, died within eight days of each other. Nevertheless, fifty years later Zwemer looked back on this period and wrote, "The sheer joy of it all comes back. Gladly would I do it all over again."[27]

Missionaries are not heroes who can boast in great sacrifice for God. They are the true Christian Hedonists. They know that the battle cry of Christian Hedonism is missions. They have discovered a hundred times more joy and satisfaction in a life devoted to Christ and the gospel than in a life devoted to frivolous comforts and pleasures and worldly advancements. Suffering, disappointment, loss—yes. But all outweighed by the superior promise of all that God is for them in Jesus. They have taken to heart the rebuke of Jesus: Beware of a self-pitying spirit of sacrifice! Missions is gain! Hundredfold gain!

On January 8, 1956, five Auca Indians of Ecuador killed Jim Elliot and his four missionary companions as they were trying to bring the gospel to the Aucas. Four young wives lost husbands and nine children lost their fathers. Elisabeth Elliot wrote that the world called it a nightmare of tragedy. Then she added, "The world did not recognize the truth of the second clause in Jim Elliot's credo":

> He is no fool who gives what he cannot keep to gain what he cannot lose.[28]

God has not put Jim Elliot and Samuel Zwemer and Lottie Moon in the world simply to picture their joyful tribulation, but also to awaken our passion for imitation. He said in Hebrews 13:7, "Consider the outcome of their life, and imitate their faith," (RSV) and in Hebrews 6:12, "[Be] imitators of those who through faith and patience inherit the promises" (RSV). Therefore, if you find in your soul a longing for the kind of satisfaction in God that freed these saints for the sacrifice of love, savor it, and stoke its embers with prayer before Satan snuffs it out. This may be a decisive moment in your life.

A FINAL CALL

Christian Hedonism is the call of God to embrace the risk and the reality of suffering for the joy that it set before us. Christ *chose* suffering, it didn't just happen to Him. He chose it as the way to create and perfect the church. He calls us to take up our cross and follow Him on the Calvary road and deny ourselves and make sacrifices for the sake of ministering to the church and presenting His sufferings to the world. But never forget, as Jonathan Edwards preached in 1723, "Self-denial destroys the very root and foundation of sorrow."[29]

The answer to this call is a radical step of Christian Hedonism. We do not choose suffering simply because it is the right thing to do, but because the One who tells us to describes it as the path to everlasting joy. He beckons us into the obedience of suffering not to demonstrate the strength of our devotion to duty, nor to reveal the vigor of our moral resolve, nor to prove the heights of our tolerance for pain; but rather to manifest, in childlike faith, the infinite preciousness of His all-satisfying promises.

In the pursuit of joy through suffering, we magnify the all-satisfying worth of the Source of our joy.

This is the essence of Christian Hedonism. In the pursuit of joy through suffering, we magnify the all-satisfying worth of the Source of our joy. Jesus Christ Himself shines as the brightness at the end of our tunnel of pain. He is the goal and the ground of our joy in suffering. Therefore the Christ-exalting meaning of our suffering is this: Christ is gain! O world, wake up and see, Christ is gain!

The chief end of man is to glorify God. It is more true in suffering than anywhere else that *God is most glorified in us when we are most satisfied in Him.* My prayer, therefore, is that the Holy Spirit would pour out on His people around the world a passion for the supremacy of our Lord and God, Jesus Christ. The pursuit of joy in Christ, whatever the pain, is a powerful testimony to Christ's supreme and all-satisfying worth. And so may it come to pass that all the peoples of the world will see the beauty of Christ, the image of God, and magnify His grace in the gladness of saving faith.

Endnotes

1. Augustine, *Confessions,* trans. R. S. Pine-Coffin (New York: Penguin Books, 1961), 21 (I, 1).
2. C. S. Lewis, *A Mind Awake: An Anthology of C. S. Lewis,* ed. Clyde Kilby (New York: Harcourt Brace and World, 1968), 22.
3. Ibid., 22–3.
4. Augustine, *Confessions,* 181 (IX, 1).
5. Blaise Pascal, *Pascal's Pensées,* trans. W. F. Trotter (New York: E. P. Dutton, 1958), 113 (thought #425).
6. Richard Baxter, *The Saints' Everlasting Rest* (Grand Rapids, Mich.: Baker Book House, 1978), 17.
7. Matthew Henry, *Commentary on the Whole Bible,* vol. 2 (Old Tappan, N.J.: Fleming H. Revel, n.d., original 1708), 1096.
8. Jonathan Edwards, *The End for Which God Created the World,* in John Piper, *God's Passion for His Glory* (Wheaton, Ill.: Crossway Books, 1998), 158, paragraph 72.
9. Jonathan Edwards, *The "Miscellanies" (Entry Nos. a-z, aa-zz, 1-500),* ed. Thomas Schafer, *The Works of*

Jonathan Edwards, vol. 13 (New Haven, Conn.: Yale University Press, 1994), 199 (Miscellany #3).

10. C. S. Lewis, *The Weight of Glory and Other Addresses* (Grand Rapids, Mich.: Eerdmans, 1965), 1–2.

11. Cited in Samuel Zwemer, "The Glory of the Impossible," in *Perspectives on the World Christian Movement*, 3rd edition, eds. Ralph Winter and Steven Hawthorne (Pasadena, Calif.: William Carey Library, 1999), 315.

12. From a letter to Sheldon Vanauken in Vanauken's *A Severe Mercy* (New York: Harper and Row, 1977), 189.

13. E. J. Carnell, *Christian Commitment* (New York: Macmillan, 1967), 160–1.

14. *Propitiation* is a rare word today. It has been replaced in many translations with more common words *(expiation, atoning sacrifice)*. I keep it in order to stress the original meaning, namely, that what Christ did by dying on the cross for sinners was to appease the wrath of God against sinners. By requiring of His Son such humiliation and suffering for the sake of God's glory, He openly demonstrated that He does not sweep sin under the rug. All contempt for His glory is duly punished, either on the cross, where the wrath of God is propitiated for those who believe, or in hell where the wrath of God is poured out on those who don't.

15. Jonathan Edwards, *The "Miscellanies," a–500,* ed. Thomas Schafer, *The Works of Jonathan Edwards,* vol. 13 (New Haven, Conn.: Yale University Press, 1994), 495. Miscellany #448; see also #87, 251–2; #332, 410; #679 (not in the New Haven volume). Emphasis added. These Miscellanies were the private notebooks of Edwards from which he built his books, such as *The End for Which God Created the World.* I have changed some punctuation from the Yale edition.

16. C. S. Lewis, *The Weight of Glory and Other Addresses,* 1–2.

17. C. S. Lewis, *Reflections on the Psalms* (New York: Harcourt, Brace and World, 1958), 94–5.

18. Jonathan Edwards, *Treatise Concerning the Religious Affections* in *The Works of Jonathan Edwards,* vol. 1 (Edinburgh: The Banner of Truth Trust, 1974), 237.

19. Joy (Psalm 100:2; Philippians 4:4; 1 Thessalonians 5:16; Romans 12:8, 12, 15), hope (Psalm 42:5; 1 Peter 1:13), fear (Luke 12:5; Romans 11:20; 1 Peter 1:17), peace (Colossians 3:15), zeal (Romans 12:11), grief (Romans 12:15; James 4:9), desire (1 Peter 2:2), tenderheartedness (Ephesians 4:32), brokenness and contrition (Psalm 51:17), gratitude (Ephesians 5:20; Colossians 3:17), lowliness (Philippians 2:3).

20. Augustine, *Confessions,* 40 (X, xxix).

21. Jonathan Edwards, *The End for Which God Created the World,* 177, paragraph 119.

22. A Native American proverb. See Guy A. Zona, ed., *The Soul Would Have No Rainbow if the Eye Had No Tears: And Other Native American Proberbs* (New York: Touchstone Books, 1994).

23. Ralph Winter, "Reconsecration to a Wartime, not a Peacetime, Lifestyle," in *Perspectives on the World Christian Movement,* 3rd edition, eds. Ralph Winter and Steven Hawthorne (Pasadena, Calif.: William Carey Library, 1999), 705.

24. Cited in Samuel Zwemer, "The Glory of the Impossible," in *Perspectives on the World Christian Movement,* 3rd edition, eds. Ralph Winter and Steven Hawthorne (Pasadena, Calif.: William Carey Library, 1999), 315.

25. For stories of the joyful sufferings of missionary saints, see John Piper, *Let the Nations Be Glad: The Supremacy of God in Missions* (Grand Rapids, Mich.: Baker Book House, 1993), 71–112.

26. Cited in Ruth Tucker, *From Jerusalem to Irian Jaya* (Grand Rapids, Mich.: Zondervan, 1983), 237. Charlotte Diggs (Lottie) Moon was born in 1840 in Virginia and sailed for China as a Baptist missionary in 1873. She is known not only for her pioneering work

in China, but also for her mobilizing the women of the Southern Baptist Church for the missionary cause.

27. Cited in *From Jerusalem to Irian Jaya,* 277.

28. Elisabeth Elliot, *Shadow of the Almighty: The Life and Testament of Jim Elliot* (New York: Harper and Brothers, 1958), 19.

29. Jonathan Edwards, "The Pleasantness of Religion," in *The Sermons of Jonathan Edwards: A Reader* (New Haven, Conn.: Yale University Press, 1999), 19.

DO YOU WANT TO
KNOW MORE?

This little book is a condensed version of *Desiring God: Meditations of a Christian Hedonist* from Multnomah Publishers, 1996. If your appetite has been wakened to go deeper into the vision of God called Christian Hedonism, I invite you to get the larger book and read it.

As the years go by, I continue to test and refine this vision with Scripture and life. If you want to see the fruit of this refining, you may look into the way Christian Hedonism relates to the nature of God (*The Pleasures of God*, revised and expanded, Multnomah, 2000), the excellence of Jesus Christ (*Seeing and Savoring Jesus Christ*,

Crossway, 2001), the gravity and gladness of preaching (*The Supremacy of God in Preaching*, Baker Book House, 1990), the power and the price of world evangelization (*Let the Nations Be Glad*, Baker, 1993), the meaning of manhood and womanhood (*What's the Difference?*, Crossway Books, 2001), the daily battle against unbelief and sin (*The Purifying Power of Living by Faith in FUTURE GRACE*, Multnomah, 1995), the discipline of prayer and fasting (*A Hunger for God*, Crossway, 1997), the lives of great saints (*The Legacy of Sovereign Joy* and *The Hidden Smile of God*, Crossway, 2000 and 2001), the foundational life and thought of Jonathan Edwards (*God's Passion for His Glory*, Crossway, 1998), and the dozens of nitty-gritty issues that we face in daily life (*A Godward Life, Books One* and *Two*, Multnomah, 1997, 1999).

There is also a ministry extension of the church I serve called *Desiring God Ministries*. On the next two pages is a word from this ministry.

DESIRING GOD.ORG

Desiring God Ministries exists to spread a passion for the supremacy of God in all things for the joy of all peoples. We have many resources available for this purpose, most of which are books, sermons, and audio collections by John Piper. Visit our Web site and discover:

- free access to over twenty years of printed sermons by John Piper,
- new free downloadable audio sermons posted weekly,
- many free articles and reviews,
- a comprehensive on-line store where you may purchase John Piper's books and audio collections, as well as God-centered children's curricula published by DGM,

- information about DGM's conferences and international offices,
- Bethlehem Conference for pastors,
- conferences for children's ministries workers.

Designed for individuals with no available discretionary funds, DGM has a *whatever-you-can-afford* policy. Contact us at an address or phone number below if you would like more information about this policy.

DESIRING GOD MINISTRIES
720 Thirteenth Ave. South
Minneapolis, Minnesota
55415-1793

Toll-free in the USA:
1-888-346-4700

International calls:
(612) 373-0651

Fax: (612) 338-4372
mail@desiringGOD.org
www.desiringGOD.org

DESIRING GOD MINISTRIES
UNITED KINGDOM
Unit 2B Spencer House
14–22 Spencer Road
Londonderry
Northern Ireland
BT47 6AA
United Kingdom

Tel/fax: 028 71342907
dgm.uk@ntlworld.com

More Faithbuilders from Piper

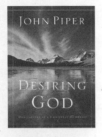

DESIRING GOD

Scripture reveals that the great business of life is to glorify God by enjoying Him forever. John Piper shows that the debate between duty and delight does not truly exist: delight *is* our duty.
ISBN 1-59052-119-6

More than 225,000 in print!

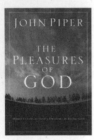

THE PLEASURES OF GOD

Fully understanding the joy of God will draw you into an encounter with His overflowing, self-replenishing, all encompassing grace—the source of living water that all Christians desire to drink.
ISBN 1-57673-665-2

FUTURE GRACE

This book helps readers discover the key to overcoming sin and living a life that honors God. John Piper encourages believers to look ahead to the grace God provides for us on a day-by-day, moment-by-moment basis.
ISBN 1-59052-191-9

BIG CHANGE

SMALL BOOKS
BIG CHANGE

w w w . b i g c h a n g e m o m e n t s . c o m

BIG CHANGE

SMALL BOOKS
BIG CHANGE